Non-Fiction and Fiction Writing for 7–11 years

IGNITING WRITING

4

Pie Corbett • Sue Palmer • Ann Webley

™Nelson Thornes
a Wolters Kluwer business

Published in 2006 by:
Nelson Thornes Ltd
Delta Place
27 Bath Road
CHELTENHAM
GL53 7TH
United Kingdom

08 09 10 / 10 9 8 7 6 5 4 3

A catalogue record for this book is available from the British Library

ISBN 978 0 7487 9732 5

Illustrations by Tom Bamfield and Can Studios
Page make-up by Pantek Arts, Maidstone, Kent

Printed in Croatia by Zrinski

Contents

Introduction

The *Igniting Writing* whiteboard sequences will help you learn more about writing. When you are working independently this book will remind you how to:

- think about what to include

- plan your work

- decide how to organise your writing in sections or paragraphs

- choose the right sorts of words and sentences for the kind of writing you are doing

- edit and improve your work when you have finished.

Contents of the CDs

CD 1: Journeys	
Sequence	**Text type**
Theme: Quests	
Story of a Quest	Story
Dispatches from a Quest	Letter writing
Scenes from a Quest	Playscript
Theme: Jets	
The Jet Engine	Explanation
Air Safety	Instructions
Jet Travel: Good or Bad?	Persuasion (L) Discussion (U)
Theme: Pilgrimages	
The Annual Hajj	Diary
Hindu Pilgrimages	Poetry
A Visit to Jerusalem	Recount
Theme: Space Travel	
Guide to the Planet Marco	Report
Outer Space, Outer Mind	Website/Advert
Finding Blue	Science fiction story

CD 2: Waterworlds	
Sequence	**Text type**
Theme: Titanic	
The Biggest and Best	Information text
The Sinking of the Titanic	Newspaper report
Water, Ice and Reflections	Poetry
Theme: Shipwreck!	
Diary of a Cabin Boy	Diary
Shipwreck	Narrative
Water Cycle	Explanation (U)
Theme: Atlantis	
Atlantis – A Perfect World	Brochure
The Search for Atlantis	Story
Atlantis Found!	Playscript
Theme: Creatures of the Deep	
The Great White Shark	Report
Dolphins – our Best Friend?	Persuasion
Does the Loch Ness Monster Exist?	Discussion

Writing fiction

To make it easier for you to use this book, the different aspects of fiction writing are broken down into separate sections. Good writers, however, weave together all they know about character, setting and plot, and may even give you information about all three in the same sentence.

Look carefully at the extract below.

'This is it lads!' The excitement was clear in Rob Watson's voice. 'Loads of people have tried to find the Lost City of Atlantis but no one has succeeded – until now.'

'How can you be sure?' Dan asked.

Rob sighed. 'I've explained before, Danny. Plato wrote about it. He said there was a plain and some high mountains. These days we have special ways of taking photos of what's under the sea. The shapes we saw look very like Plato described.' He jumped up and ran over to the side. 'We're there all right!'

His elder son Alex looked up from the dive masks he was cleaning and frowned. 'That's all very well, Dad, but have you forgotten the warning?'

Key: Information about character
       Information about setting
       Information about plot

Can you see how the writer has threaded together the elements of story writing in this short extract? Dialogue is used to move the plot forward, but it also tells you about the characters and the setting. The characters' actions move the plot forwards, but also reveal their personalities. The setting is integral to this story, as it sets the scene for an adventure or suspense story.

Different types of stories will emphasise different aspects of story writing. An action/adventure/suspense story, like the one above, will probably use a lot of dialogue. A story about issues or characters' feelings may focus more on how the main character feels. A fantasy or science fiction story would probably give more detail on the setting. Think carefully about the type of story you are writing, and the effect that you want your writing to have, as you craft your work.

Finally, all good writers edit their stories. Always go back to your work and take time to improve it.

Characters

Getting ideas

Think of someone that you know, have seen or met. Try thinking of unusual or interesting people. If you are writing an historical story, decide whether you are going to invent a fictitious character, or base your character on a real person. You can also use pictures, look through newspapers and magazines, or download pictures of historical characters from websites.

1. Decide on a name.

   Reuse a name that fits in with the period about which you are writing, e.g. Sanctus Cabot.

2. Think of a few details to describe your character. This will help the reader be able to 'see' the character.
   - Wearing earrings: perhaps a precious farewell gift? What might they mean to the character?
   - Expression of determination – but perhaps also anxiety?
   - Speech: likely to be formal.
   - Writing a journal or diary. Suggests he is thoughtful?

3. Decide how your character is feeling, e.g.

   > hopeful, anxious, homesick, excited, worried

Building your character

- Use others' reactions and comments.
- Reveal your character's thoughts, e.g. *Sancto wondered whether he would ever see his brothers or mother again.*
- Let an adult or the author comment on events.
- Contrast the opening and ending to show how the main character has changed.
- Show what the main character has learned, e.g. *Then, with hope in his heart, he shouldered his sack and followed his father away from Grates Cove, heading south, towards who knows what or where. Towards hope.*
- Show events through different characters' eyes.
- Have contrasting characters.
- Show what a character feels inside whilst pretending something else on the outside, e.g. *Fighting back the tears, Sancto stood up and filled his water bottle. He did not want his father to see any sign of what he felt was weakness.*

WRITER'S TOOLKIT

To develop your characters, ask questions about them:

- ✔ How old are they?
- ✔ What are they interested in?
- ✔ Do they have anything they really dislike?
- ✔ Have they a special talent?
- ✔ Do they have a secret?
- ✔ What are they afraid of?
- ✔ What is their biggest wish?

LANGUAGE TOOLKIT

What do your characters look like?

- ✔ Use a few **details** to suggest what a character is like, e.g. *He paused and stared at his reflection. Everyone said that he looked like his mother's side of the family.* (Suggests that his mother is important to him; that he misses her.)
- ✔ Describe with a **list**, e.g. *The sailor had thin grey hair, bloodshot eyes and lines that criss-crossed his face.*
- ✔ Use well-chosen **adjectives** and **similes**, e.g. *They looked like crows picking at the sand, caught in the wind's teeth.*
- ✔ Mention a **distinctive feature**, e.g. *He wore ornate Venetian earrings.*

Show how they feel through what they say.

- ✔ Reflect their **personality/feelings**, e.g. *'Leave me alone!'*
- ✔ Use **expressions**, powerful **verbs** and **adverbs**, e.g. *'There! Now you look just like a real pirate,' she laughed, as she gave him the earrings.*
- ✔ Add in a supporting **action**, e.g. *'We'll need an axe,' said John Cabot, clapping his old friend on the shoulder.*
- ✔ Avoid a string of dialogue.

Show how they feel by what they do.

- ✔ Reflect the character's **feelings**, e.g. *In the cold dark of the cave he whispered 'goodnight' and crept back under his tarpaulin.*
- ✔ Make sure different character types behave in different ways.
- ✔ Use powerful **verbs** and **adverbs**, especially for movement (*amble, shuffle, dash*) and for looking (*peer, glance, stare, glare*).

Settings

1. **What sort of story are you going to write?**

   Before you can think about creating a setting, you need to think about the type of story you are writing. Make a list of possible settings. You might find it helpful to refer to the list of story types on page 23.

2. **Where do I begin?**

   - **Picture it:** Try using a photograph, picture or drawing to help with thinking about the setting. Label the picture with descriptive words or phrases. Remember that your reader will not see the picture, so use details and be precise.

   - **Draw it:** Draw a map or landscape of your story setting. This is a good way of creating a setting for a fantasy or sci-fi story.

   - **Sense it:** Close your eyes and imagine you are standing in your setting. What can you hear, smell and feel? What time of day is it? What is the weather like?

   - **Film it:** Imagine you are filming your setting. What can you see through the lens? How does the perspective change as you zoom in to focus on details, or pan out to see the whole scene?

   - **Now write it:**

     Zak left the shed and went back into the base for his evening meal. The sun had set by the time he had finished. High above him, Mini and Maxi, the twin moons of Marco, glowed. One was a tiny, silvery, purple dot and the other like a huge, orange balloon. They cast an eerie light. Zak crept round to the shed, hoping that no-one would spot him.

   ## Remember!

   Weave the setting description into the story by linking it to how the characters feel and what they do and say. Change the setting to create a different mood. To create suspense use a lonely, dark setting.

WRITER'S TOOLKIT

✔ Choose an interesting name for your setting.

✔ Think about the time of day and weather.

✔ Show the setting through the main character's eyes, e.g. Zak could see a bright speck in the sky which grew bigger and bigger. What could it be?

✔ Use unexpected detail as a 'hook', e.g. It was then that he noticed it. Something had been crawling in the fine, red dust beneath the largest tower. Zak stooped down and stared at the marks. They were not like anything he had ever seen.

✔ Change the setting to create atmosphere, e.g. the path grew darker ...

LANGUAGE TOOLKIT

Have you used:

✔ powerful **verbs** and **adjectives**, e.g. stars <u>speckled</u> the <u>night</u> sky

✔ **similes**, e.g. like a huge, <u>orange balloon</u>, the moon

✔ **metaphors**, e.g. the <u>wall's backbone</u> stretched across the land

✔ **personification**, e.g. the wind moaned

✔ **lists**? e.g. He stared at the dusty chairs, broken machines and old boxes

Creating plots

Getting ideas

A good storywriter is always on the lookout for a story idea. You need a story built around a 'problem'. You might get ideas from:

- stories that you have read
- story tapes
- retelling or changing traditional tales, nursery rhymes or story poems
- things that happen to you
- anecdotes.

Start by mixing together your ingredients:

- **Who** is the main character?
- **Where** is he/she?
- **What** is he/she doing?
- **What** is going to go wrong?
- **How** will it be sorted out?
- **How** will it end?

Story patterns

It can help if you use a basic pattern for your writing. To see a list of different types of stories, plus their plot features, look on page 23. Here are some suggestions for basic plot ideas:

- overcoming a problem
- quest/journey
- conquer the monster
- character flaw
- warning
- lost/found
- suspense
- wishing
- catastrophe
- magical
- stories with a moral
- changing (sad – happy, poor – rich, weak over strong, good over evil)
- traditional pattern.

How to plan

Start working out the plot by jotting down ideas. Keep the plot simple and drive towards the end. Here are some devices that can help with your planning.

Flowcharts

A flowchart is ideal for planning a play or a story that has a set number of scenes.

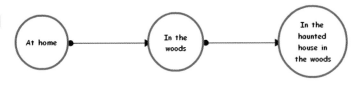

Timelines

A timeline is helpful for planning a letter or a diary. It allows you to put events in chronological order.

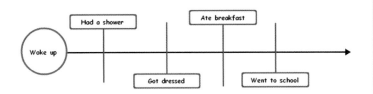

Storyboards

A storyboard is a good way of planning if you like to visualise each scene. It allows you to use a combination of words and pictures to map out your story.

Story picture maps

You might find a story picture map useful if you are writing a science fiction or fantasy story. It enables you to create the setting and the plot together, in a visual way.

Story mountain

Use a story mountain to build excitement or interest into your storyline. A good plot should have moments of suspense or crisis, or the characters should be faced with a problem or challenge.

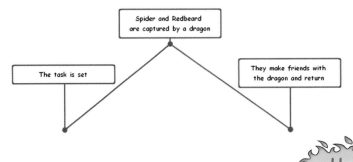

WRITER'S TOOLKIT

Have you:

✔ used your plan to help you write your story

✔ made any changes, and have they added to your original idea

✔ controlled the dialogue, or is there too much

✔ balanced the action, dialogue and description

✔ made the story well-paced or have you rushed any part

✔ used the settings to create different atmospheres

✔ shown what the main character is like by what they say and do

✔ written an ending that shows how the main character feels or what has been learned?

LANGUAGE TOOLKIT

Have you:

✔ stayed in the same **tense**

✔ stayed in the same **person**, e.g. I, or *he/she*

✔ used connectives to link ideas, sentences and make paragraph changes? e.g.

> Once upon a time; One day; Suddenly, so, Finally

Remember!

Different story types may use different patterns, e.g.
- traditional – patterns of three (three tasks, three brothers)
- mystery – only understood at the end
- fantasy – often involving a quest.

Muddling story types can create comedy, e.g. rewriting *Cinderella* as a modern soap opera.

Writing dialogue

WRITER'S TOOLKIT

✔ Use the dialogue to show something about the characters' feelings or personalities.

✔ Use the dialogue to move the action forwards, e.g. 'Let's go to the pond now,' said Bill.

✔ Have characters discussing events.

✔ Have characters discussing other characters.

✔ Listen to the sorts of things people say and steal ideas!

✔ Collect expressions.

✔ Show what a character is doing while they speak by adding information, e.g. 'Hey,' said Billi, picking up the sword.

LANGUAGE TOOLKIT

✔ Put what is said inside **speech marks**.

✔ Put any **punctuation** inside the speech marks, e.g.

'Look out!' said Shasta.
'Why?' asked Tizer.

✔ Use powerful **speech verbs**, e.g. 'Look,' shouted Shasta.

✔ Use 'said' plus an **adverb**, e.g. 'Look,' Shasta said miserably.

✔ Start a **new line** whenever a new speaker speaks.

✔ You can put the speaker **before** or **after** direct speech, e.g. Sandil said, 'When do we arrive?; 'When do we arrive?' asked Sandil.

Using paragraphs

Why do we need paragraphs?

Paragraphs help writers to organise their thoughts or ideas. They also make it easier for the reader to follow the storyline.

Planning paragraphs

Once you have worked out your plot, try building the paragraphs into your plan. You could do this by using boxes in a flowchart. In this way a paragraph is rather like a 'scene' in a film. It usually contains one event.

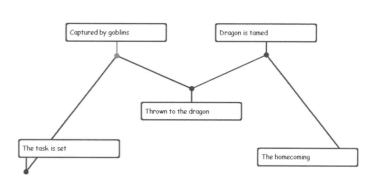

When to change paragraphs

Use this table to help you to work out when a new paragraph is needed:

When?	Why?	Example
A new person speaks	To show that it is a different speaker.	'Hello,' said Daisy. 'Hi there,' replied Poppy, ignoring her.
Place	To show that the action has shifted to another place.	In the next room …
Time	To let the reader know that time has passed.	The next morning …
Person	To introduce a new person or to move the attention to a different character.	Bill dashed in …
Surprising events	This is used when a dramatic, unexpected or exciting event occurs.	There was a crash …
Mood	To show that the mood has changed. A change in mood can also be shown by introducing a different sort of weather, or by altering the time of day.	The clouds darkened …
Viewpoint	To reveal the thoughts of a different character, or to show events from a different character's point of view.	However, Sancto had a different idea …

WRITER'S TOOLKIT

The main types of paragraph are:

✔ **opening** – set the scene, introduce the main character

✔ **build-up** – get the story going; your character is doing something

✔ **dilemma** – something goes wrong; there is a problem to solve

✔ **resolution** – solving the problem to make everything ok

✔ **ending** – show what has been learned or how a character has changed.

You may also need an action paragraph for the exciting part of the story. A suspense paragraph is also useful to keep the reader on the edge of their seat! Use a time-slip paragraph when you want the main character to go back in time. Cliff-hangers are handy for keeping the reader wanting to read on, to find out if everything will be ok.

LANGUAGE TOOLKIT

Have you used:

✔ **connectives** to open paragraphs, e.g. — Later that day …

✔ **punchy openings**, e.g. — Shasta screamed!

✔ **question openings**, e.g. — Was he hurt?

✔ **scene-setters**, e.g. — The thunder rumbled.

✔ **character openings**, e.g. — Brad banged his head.

✔ **connectives** to link ideas within paragraphs? e.g. — as, so, but, after, before, when, while, that, and

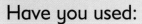
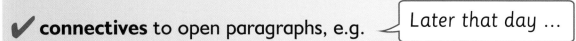

Style

A good writer knows that how they say something is just as important as what they say. In other words, you could make the most interesting plot sound boring if your style is dull and plodding.

Developing your writing style

Good writing style means:
- choosing good words
- varying your sentences.

Remember to link the story together so that the reader can follow what is happening. This means staying in the same tense, using pronouns and connectives.

Choosing good words

It is worth keeping a writing journal and collecting words to use. Notice well-chosen words when you are reading and store them away. Think about using words that add something new for the reader, and that add surprise. Try to choose words that will illuminate the subject.

Varying your sentences

Build up a store of different types of sentences. Invent sentences that might be handy for different reasons. Jot these in your writing journal. Notice how good writers vary their sentences. Try copying different sentence patterns and using these in your own writing. Read your sentences aloud and think about what they sound like and their meaning. Try to write powerfully. Try rewriting a sentence to see if you can improve it; try changing words, try adding similes, metaphors or alliteration. See the table below.

Technique	How it works	Example
Questions	To make the reader wonder what has or will happen.	Where was it?
Exclamations	To add impact.	Help!
Simple sentences	To say what is happening in clear, straightforward language.	The alien winked at me.
Compound sentences	To make the writing flow.	The dragon snorted and ate its dinner.
Complex sentences	To use when, how or where to add in extra information.	As the dwarf stood up, the sword glowed.
Sentence of three for description	To build up a picture in the reader's mind.	He stared at the alien's green boots, golden eyes and purple hands.
Sentence of three for action	To speed up the action.	The dragon sneezed, shook its head and then began to cry.
Drop in a chunk	To add in information.	Sancto, hoping for the best, ran home.
Tag on a chunk	To add another idea.	Zak ran home, waving to his friends.

WRITER'S TOOLKIT

Try to vary the **openings** to sentences:

✔ How? – *Calmly, she walked on …*

✔ Where? – *Under the hill was a mine …*

✔ When? – *After that, they went home …*

✔ Use similes, e.g. *Like an eagle he swooped.*

✔ Use an 'ing' clause, e.g. *Laughing loudly, they …*

✔ Use an 'ed' clause, e.g. *Exhausted by running, the magician …*

✔ Use one word, e.g. *Sad, he sat down.*

LANGUAGE TOOLKIT

Have you used:

✔ precise **nouns**, e.g. — Canary **not** bird

✔ a **noun phrase**, e.g. — The elegant canary from next-door

✔ well-chosen **adjectives**, e.g. — rusty letter box **not** red letter box

✔ powerful **verbs**, e.g. — rushed **not** went

✔ well-chosen **adverbs**, e.g. — cautiously, he opened …

✔ **similes**, e.g. — like a giant

✔ **alliteration**, e.g. — trees tussled

✔ **metaphors**, e.g. — cloudy eyes

✔ **personification**, e.g. — the moon grinned

✔ **onomatopoeia**? e.g. — the wood cracked

Poetry

Gather your ideas

Poets find ideas in many ways:

- listening to music
- looking at art work
- day dreaming
- doodling
- looking at photographs
- drawing before writing
- reflecting on a personal experience.

When writing poetry, first of all, you need to decide what you are going to write about. Here are some tips that you might find helpful.

1. If you don't know where to begin, try the following:
   - Look carefully at your subject.
   - Use your memory.
   - Think about what you can see/hear/smell/taste/touch as you look at or think about something.
   - See what happens if you put two unrelated ideas or objects together.

2. Start jotting down words, thoughts and ideas. You could make:
   - notes
   - a word hoard
   - a word list
   - a mind map.

Organise your ideas

Now you can organise your ideas into a form. Look at the table of different types of poems on page 23.

WRITER'S TOOLKIT

Create pictures in your poems by using:

✔ similes, e.g. **as** dark **as** space; **like** a moon

✔ metaphors, e.g. the owl stood stump still

✔ personification, e.g. the trees shivered.

Create sounds in your poems by using:

✔ alliteration, e.g. a snake slipped by

✔ onomatopoeia, e.g. bees buzzed

✔ rhyme for performance, e.g. Running fast/got to last

Revise your writing by:

✔ deleting words

✔ adding words

✔ changing words

✔ reorganising words

✔ using alliteration/similes, etc.

✔ trying different forms.

LANGUAGE TOOLKIT

Have you used:

✔ precise **nouns**, e.g. poodle **not** dog

✔ powerful **verbs**, e.g. snapped **not** said

✔ well-chosen **adjectives**, e.g. rusty letter box **not** red letter box

✔ well-chosen **adverbs**, e.g. cautiously

✔ new **word combinations**, e.g. wolf fur smoke

✔ **compressed language**, e.g. thin heron, **not** the heron was thin

✔ **repetition** for effect?

Playscripts

Where to start?

A play is a story that is performed by actors. You could begin by taking a story that you know well and turning it into a play. Or you could use characters from a story and develop further scenes. Consider starting by putting a character into a situation, and then thinking about how they would react. It can help to begin by role-playing or improvising and seeing what develops.

What sort of play do you want to put on?

Think about how much time you have and where you could perform your play. Decide on the type of performance:

- play
- video
- puppet show
- musical
- radio drama
- sketch.

Decide on the purpose of your play:

- Is it to make the audience laugh or cry?
- Is it to make them understand something?
- Do you want to scare or frighten them?
- Is it to teach them a lesson?

Remember!

All audiences will want to be entertained.

Ask yourself if you need:

- scenery
- props
- costumes
- make-up
- lighting
- sound effects.

For more information on planning and structuring your plot, refer to page 10.

For more information on building believable characters, refer to page 6.

For guidance on creating a setting, refer to page 8.

WRITER'S TOOLKIT

✔ List the characters at the start of the play.

✔ Longer plays are divided into acts, which are separated by intervals. Each act is made up of a number of scenes.

✔ Start by describing the scene and what the characters are doing in italics/brackets. Write this in the present tense as 'stage directions'.

✔ Put the name of the speaker on the left. Use a colon to separate the characters' names from what they say.

✔ Insert occasional character directions to suggest how something should be spoken, especially if it is not obvious.

✔ Put stage directions in italics/brackets to show what characters should do, if it is not obvious but is important.

✔ Dialogue is the most important aspect of a play. It moves the plot forwards, tells you more about the characters, and it can even give information about the setting.

✔ Where possible, include the use of dance, song, music or sound effects.

LANGUAGE TOOLKIT

✔ Do **not** use speech marks or speech verbs.

✔ Write your play like a **conversation**.

✔ Use **adverbs** for directions (*angrily, moving swiftly*).

✔ **Speech** may use:

- slang (*geddit?*)
- informal/formal words (*grub/food*)
- contracted forms (*don't*)
- conversational words (*wos up?*)
- everyday expressions (*don't give me grief*)
- sentence fragments (*upstairs?*).

Performers' checklist

- Speak clearly and loudly enough.
- Use plenty of expression.
- Keep in your 'role'.
- Do not stand in front of each other.
- Do not talk too quickly.
- Use gestures to show how you feel.
- Use dramatic pauses.

Creating suspense

One way of making your writing really exciting is to build in suspense. This means letting the reader think that something dreadful might be about to happen. This is how you could do it.

1. **All is well**
   First, put your character into a situation where everything is going well. Show them doing something they enjoy. In this way, you can lull the reader into a false sense of security, thinking that everything is all right, e.g.

   Jo sat down under the trees and watched as the dragonflies flitted across the pond's surface. She closed her eyes and began to drift off.

2. **Suggest that something might be about to happen**
   Introduce some suspense by having your character:
   * hear something unusual or out of place that suggests that something might happen, e.g. *he heard a creak …*
   * see a glimpse of something ominous, e.g. *a figure darted out …*

3. **Build the tension**
   When you are writing a suspense paragraph, try to see what is happening in your mind. It will need to be very 'visual' so the reader can also see what is happening. It helps if you make the scene dark and cold. It also helps if the character is alone. Try using short sentences for drama. Use a question to make the reader wonder what is happening. It is also helpful if you show the main character's reactions.

   She woke with a start. Somebody or something was creeping through the trees towards her. Cautiously, Jo stared into the dark between the trees. What was it? She shivered, but not from the cold. At that moment, she heard a hissing sound and then the flicker of a red eye. Jo gasped.

WRITER'S TOOLKIT

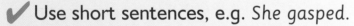

✔ Use short sentences, e.g. *She gasped.*
✔ Use powerful verbs, e.g. *creeping.*
✔ Introduce a glimpse, e.g. *the flicker of a red eye.*
✔ Introduce a sound effect, e.g. *a hissing sound.*
✔ Use 'empty' words, e.g. *something* or *somebody.*
✔ Use a question to make the reader wonder, e.g. *What was it?*
✔ Show the character's reactions, e.g. *Jo gasped.*

Story/Poetry types

Story type	Characters	Settings	Key features
Adventure	Hero, heroine, baddy	Island, cave, tunnel	Cliff hangers, action
Mystery	Detective, suspects, victim	Old house, cellar, attic	Red herrings, clues
Fantasy	Dwarf, hobbit, goblin, dragon	Enchanted forest, cloud city, lonely tower, ruined bridge	Magical events, tasks
Sci-fi	Alien, space pilot, robot, space creature	Other planets, spaceships, polluted planets, undersea world	New inventions, computers
Ghost	Ghost, frightened house owner	Deserted house, dark alley, graveyard	Suspense, unexplained events
School/home	Teacher, friends, gangs, bully	Playground, classroom, journey to school	Issues, e.g. bullying, stealing, lying
Traditional	Princess, king, ogre, magical creatures	Forest, palace, tower, market, cave	Good vs evil, events in threes, moral at end

Poem type	Features
Ballad	Formal story, poem or song in rhyming form using verses and chorus.
Performance	Entertaining poem often in rhyme.
Rap	Rapid rhyming verse often performed with music.
Narrative	Story poem; may rhyme or not, e.g. Chocolate Cake (Michael Rosen); The Highwayman (Alfred Noyes).
Limerick	Funny poem with five lines.
Nonsense	Invested words, e.g. *squirtle*; fantastical ideas; often rhyming, e.g. *Twas brillig and the slithy toves did gyre and gimble in the wabe.*
Lists	Repeated pattern or phrase, e.g. *last night I saw the moon singing, last night I saw the stars dancing.*
Shape	Poem written in the shape of the subject.
Free verse	Open pattern; adjectives; similes; metaphors; powerful verbs.
Haiku	Japanese form; usually three lines; carefully-chosen words, often 5, 7, 5 syllables.
Tanka	A haiku with two additional lines of 7 syllables.
Cinquain	Five lines; ending in a surprise using 2, 4, 6, 8, 2 syllables.
Kenning	Old English/Norse naming riddle by using pairs, e.g. *whale-road (sea).*
Concrete	Shape of poem adds to meaning.
Calligram	Letters in shape of words' meaning.
Acrostic	Subject used to spell out first, central or end line.

Non-fiction writing

There are lots of different kinds of non-fiction texts. In this book you will find **toolkits** to help you remember what to do.

Whenever you write non-fiction, remember to:

- write an **introduction** and make it clear why you are writing

- decide on the best order for your **paragraphs** – this will depend on the task and your purpose. Your writing must have an impact on the reader

- start each paragraph with a **topic sentence**

- use relevant **technical language**

- use **accurate descriptions**

- use **connectives**

- write a **conclusion** – this could involve a summing-up, a personal point of view or a general comment.

You can use the toolkits whenever you are writing, for example, literacy, history, geography or science.

Planning non-fiction writing

You can use the **skeleton diagrams** in this book to help you plan.

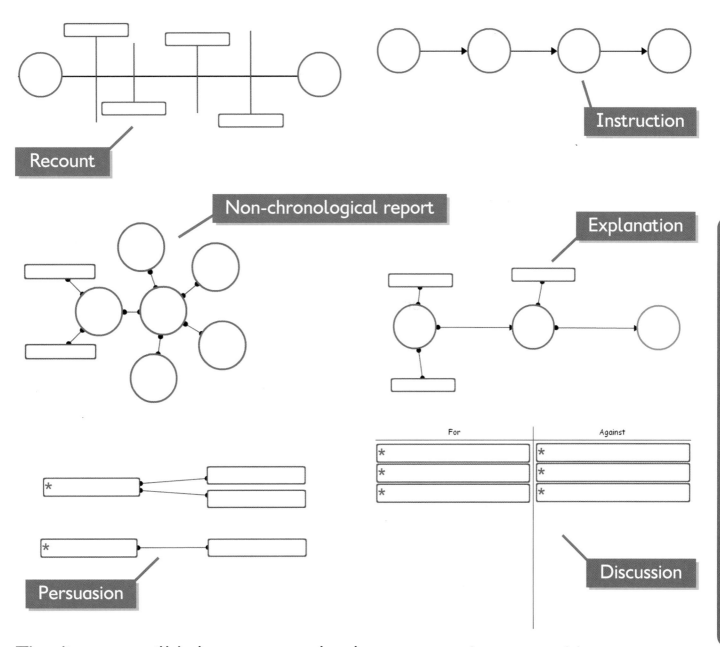

Recount

Instruction

Non-chronological report

Explanation

Persuasion

For	Against
*	*
*	*
*	*

Discussion

The diagrams will help you remember how to organise your writing.

- Add **more words** on the other lines on the diagram to show the facts or examples that you plan to write about. These are memory joggers so you can remember to write about them in detail. **Don't write in sentences**.

- Plan an **introduction** and **conclusion**.

- Think about whether you want to add anything to your writing such as:

  - diagrams

  - fact boxes

  - charts

  - sub-headings.

Now you are ready to write!

You can use the pages in this book to help you remember what to do.

Make sure you think about your **purpose** and **audience**. This will affect how you write.

Think about whether your writing will be **formal** or **informal**, or something in between. This will depend on your task and how well you know your audience.

Your writing needs to be **interesting** and **full of detail**.

Mixed text types

A lot of writing is a **mixture of text types** so you have to decide how to plan.

First decide which **skeleton diagram** will help you **organise** your work most easily.

Then you can think about the different **language features** you need. You may need to look at more than one toolkit.

Examples

- A **tourist guide** would be planned like a non-chronological report, but it would include persuasive devices to encourage people to visit. Look at how this works in 'Atlantis – a Perfect World' or 'Outer Space, Outer Mind'.

- A **newspaper report** might be mainly recount, but could have sections of explanation to make the detail clear to a reader. It could also be persuasive if the paper was trying to give an opinion about the event. The 'Sinking of the Titanic' is a good example of this.

- A **letter** might contain elements of several text types, depending upon the purpose. Look at the letters sent and received in 'Dispatches from a Quest'.

- A **non-chronological report** might need to include a section of explanation. See how this is done in 'Titanic – the Biggest and Best' or 'The Great White Shark'.

Writing recounts

Purpose

A recount tells us about something that has happened.

+

Audience

It is for someone who wants to know all about what has happened. The exact audience (and how well you know them) will depend on the task.

There are lots of different kinds of **recount**, for example:

- a write-up of a trip or activity
- an account of something that happened in history
- a newspaper article about something that happened
- a letter to tell someone about an event
- a diary or 'blog' (website diary)
- an encyclopaedia entry
- a biography or autobiography
- an account of a science experiment.

Look at the example below from 'A Visit to Jerusalem'.

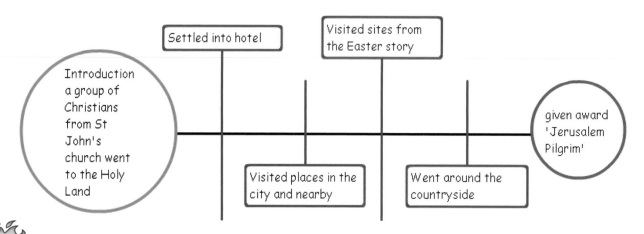

Organisation toolkit

Remember to:

- write a **title** to interest the reader
- write an **introduction** that sets the scene. You could try to answer the questions *who?*, *what?*, *where?*, *when?* and *why?* and convince the reader to read on
- write about events in **paragraphs**, organised in **chronological order**. Choose details that are amusing, exciting or significant in order to interest the reader
- start each paragraph with a **topic sentence**
- write a **conclusion**. This could comment on what happened or say something about how the people involved felt.

LANGUAGE TOOLKIT

Remember to:

✔ write in the **past tense**, except for present circumstances and feelings

✔ use **time connecting phrases** (*After the flight; over the first three days of the pilgrimage*)

✔ include the **names of people** and **places** (*Father Mark; Bethlehem*)

✔ use other **topic words** and examples of relevant **technical language** (*holy water; sermon*)

✔ use **accurate descriptions** (*three stone pillars; white cotton sheet*)

✔ use either **first person** (personal account) or **third person** (impersonal account)

✔ use **direct quotes** and/or **reported speech** where relevant. (*Pat said, 'I had not until then thought of myself as a <u>pilgrim</u> embarking on a pilgrimage, but as just an ordinary person going on a rather special holiday'.*)

Writing non-chronological reports

Purpose

A report gives factual information about a range of subjects, for example, animals, types of transport, life in Tudor times, towns.

+

Audience

It is for someone who wants to know about something.

There are lots of different kinds of **report**, for example:

- an information leaflet
- a newspaper or magazine article
- a letter
- a non-fiction book

- an encyclopaedia entry
- a catalogue
- a school website.

Look at this example from 'The Great White Shark'.

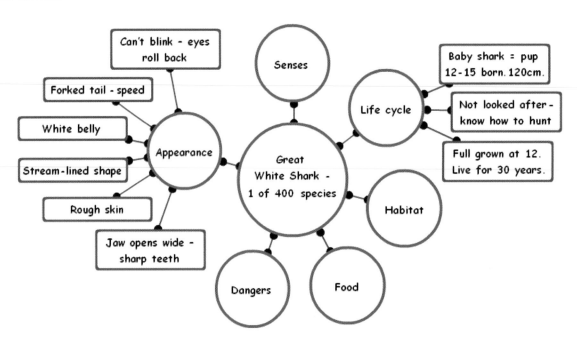

Organisation toolkit

Remember to:

- write a **title** to say what you are writing about. Try to interest the reader (*Titanic – the Biggest and the Best*)
- write an **introduction** that defines the subject. You should also try to make a statement or ask a question to interest or intrigue the reader so that they want to read on
- organise your work in to **paragraphs**, starting with a **topic sentence**. You could also use **sub-headings** to divide up your work
- write your paragraphs in any order, but think about the most sensible order, for example, in a report about an animal, describe the appearance first
- draw **diagrams**, **charts** or **fact boxes** if they help to give the information more clearly
- write a **conclusion** that draws your writing to an end
- include a **glossary** at the end, if relevant.

LANGUAGE TOOLKIT

Remember to:

- ✔ write in the **present tense** except for historical reports
- ✔ write in the **third person** (*he, she, it, they*)
- ✔ write mainly in a **formal style**, however, you might want to refer directly to the reader at the end
- ✔ use relevant **technical language** (*tenticles, skull, teeth*)
- ✔ use **accurate descriptions** to give information (*white belly, razor sharp teeth*)
- ✔ include **interesting detail** and **several facts or examples** about each part of the subject (*Astounding as it may seem a Great White might lose and replace up to 40,000 teeth during its lifetime*)
- ✔ use '**weasel words**' to cover exceptions (*usually, maybe, generally*).

Writing instructions

Purpose		Audience
Instructions tell us how to do or make something.	**+**	Instructions are for someone who needs to know how to do or make something.

There are lots of different kinds of **instructions**. Some need to be written in order, for example:

- a recipe
- an instruction poster, e.g. instructions on how to use a computer
- an instruction leaflet, e.g. on how to make a hand puppet or safety instructions on an aeroplane
- instructions for a game
- map directions.

Some **instructions** do not need to be written in order, for example:

- a list of school rules
- a poster showing advice on water safety.

Look at the example below from 'Air Safety'.

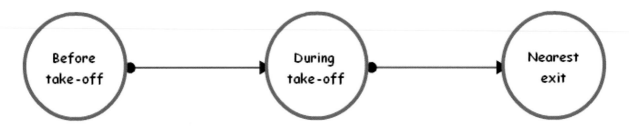

Organisation toolkit

Remember to:

- write a **title** that sets out the purpose for the instructions (Safety Instructions)
- if relevant, write an **opening** sentence directed at the reader (Follow these instructions to ensure proper safety)
- include lists of **equipment** or **ingredients**, if needed
- write the instructions as a **sequence of steps**
- use **bullet points** or **numbers** to make the order clear
- draw **diagrams** if they help to give the information more clearly
- write an **ending** sentence directed at the reader (Enjoy your flight with Flyaway Airlines).

LANGUAGE TOOLKIT

Remember to:

✔ use **imperative verbs** (<u>Put</u> seats into the upright position)

✔ use the **present tense** and **third person** for instructions

✔ use some **time connectives** (first, next)

✔ use **technical language** related to the subject (emergency exit, aisle)

✔ use **accurate descriptions** in order to make the instructions clear (Fold the <u>smaller</u> piece of paper in half)

✔ where relevant, **extend** the instruction to provide **extra advice** and **explanation** (Insert the <u>metal</u> tab into the buckle).

Non-fiction

Writing explanations

Purpose

An explanation states **how** or **why** something happens, or **how** something works.

+

Audience

It is for someone who wants to understand something.

There are lots of different kinds of **explanations**. Some are complete texts and others are parts of a mixed text, for example:

- a question and answer leaflet
- a section of explanation in a letter or newspaper article
- a non-fiction book
- an encyclopaedia entry
- a conclusion to a science experiment
- a technical manual, such as for a computer or games console.

Look at the example below from 'The Jet Engine'.

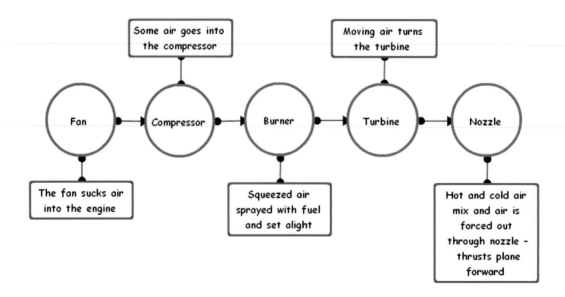

Organisation toolkit

Remember to:

- write a **title** to say what you are writing about (*The Jet Engine – how does it work?*)

- write an **introduction** to give any background information

- write your **paragraphs** in **chronological order**. Start each new section with a **topic sentence**

- draw **a diagram** if it helps make your explanation clearer

- use **bullet points** or **sub-headings** if this helps break up the explanation

LANGUAGE TOOLKIT

Remember to:

- ✔ write in the **present tense**, unless you are writing an explanation about something in the past

- ✔ write in the **third person** (*it, they*)

- ✔ use a **formal** style

- ✔ use **time connectives** to show the order clearly (*first, next, then*)

- ✔ use words to show **how** or **why** (**cause and effect**) (*because, consequently, therefore, when*)

- ✔ use **technical vocabulary**. Define any difficult words or include them in a **glossary** (*thrust, nozzle*)

- ✔ use **clear descriptions** to help explain things

- ✔ use 'weasel words' to cover generalisations (*usually, often*)

- ✔ make the explanation **interesting** for the reader.

Writing persuasion

+

Audience

It is for anyone who might be interested in the subject, but may have a different point of view. This means you have to include lots of facts and arguments to try to make them agree with you.

There are lots of different kinds of **persuasive writing**, for example:

- an advertisement
- a poster or flier
- a book 'blurb'
- a newspaper or magazine article
- a leaflet, e.g. from people who want to stop whale hunting
- a letter, e.g. from someone trying to persuade somebody to do something.

Look at the example below from 'Dolphins'.

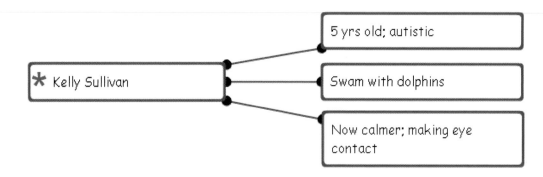

Organisation toolkit

Remember to:

- write an **eye-catching title** to say what you are writing about (*Protect the Dolphin before it is too late*)
- write an **introduction** that states the point of view to be argued
- write your points in **paragraphs**, starting with **topic sentences**. These signal the argument to be made in that paragraph
- think about what your opponents might argue and include **counter arguments**. You can either do this in each paragraph as you go along or in a paragraph at the end
- use **bullet points**, **sub-headings** and **pictures** if these help to make your points clearer or stronger
- write an **ending** that re-states your point of view.

LANGUAGE TOOLKIT

Remember to:

- write in the **present tense**
- choose **emotive language** to help give your point of view (<u>Thousands of</u> dolphins are <u>cruelly trapped</u> in fishing nets each year)
- use words to give **reasons** for your point of view (*because, so, this means that*)
- use 'dare-to-disagree' expressions to get the reader on your side. Try to appear friendly and reasonable (*There is no doubt; the time has come to INSIST that all countries pass laws to protect them from harm*)
- use **type size** and **punctuation** for effect
- use **technical vocabulary** (*tuna fishing, trawling, nets*)
- use **connecting phrases** to signal your points (<u>In addition</u>, action needs to be taken because dolphins are in great danger)
- use **alliteration** and **rhyme** if it helps the task
- use '**weasel words**' to help persuade (*probably, perhaps, often*)
- use **rhetorical questions** (*How long can this go on?*).

Non-fiction

Writing discussion

<table>
<tr><td>

Purpose

A discussion puts forward both sides of the argument. It gives points **for** and **against** as a **balanced** piece of writing.

</td><td>

+

</td><td>

Audience

It is for anyone who is interested in the subject. They might be trying to make up their mind by reading what you have written.

</td></tr>
</table>

There are lots of different kinds of **discussion writing**, for example:

- a leaflet about both sides of an issue
- a newspaper article
- information in non-fiction books
- a write-up of a debate.

Look at the example from 'Loch Ness'.

Does the Loch Ness monster exist?

For (Nicky)	Against (Adam)
* Sightings & photos	* Sightings & photos
* Expedition	* No scientific proof
* Don't have to see to believe	* Conditions in loch

Organisation toolkit

Remember to:

- write a **title** to say what you are writing about (*Jet travel out, or keep it?*)
- write an **introduction** that states what the discussion is about (*There are many stories of sightings of a monster in Loch Ness in Scotland. However, people disagree about whether it exists or not*)
- organise the main part of the discussion in one of two ways:
  1. First write about all the arguments **for** the case. Write one **paragraph** for each point and begin each new point with a **topic sentence**. Then write about the arguments **against** the case. Write one **paragraph** for each point and begin each new point with a **topic sentence**
  2. Present each argument and counter-argument in a separate **paragraph**, which starts with a **topic sentence**
- write a **conclusion** that sums up the argument and gives a reasoned opinion.

LANGUAGE TOOLKIT

Remember to:

- ✔ write in the **present tense**
- ✔ write in the **third** person
- ✔ use **technical vocabulary** (pollution, greenhouse gases, climate change)
- ✔ use words to show **reasons** (because, so)
- ✔ use **descriptions** to help make the facts clear
- ✔ use words to signal **both sides** of the argument (on the one hand environmentalists point out, some people argue, others believe, however supporters of the monster theory say)
- ✔ use **connecting phrases** to signal your points (first of all, in addition)
- ✔ use '**weasel words**' to help back up a point (probably, perhaps, often)
- ✔ give **examples** to back up what you say.

Writing letters

Purpose

There are lots of reasons for writing a letter, for example, to keep in touch with someone, to send news, to complain, to congratulate, to persuade, to reply to a previous letter, to ask for information or to explain something.

Letters can involve different **text types**. This means you will need to use parts of the other **toolkits** in this book to help you write your letter.

+

Audience

Your audience could be a friend or relation (a **personal** letter) or someone you don't know (a **formal** letter).

Personal letter

Dear Bramble,

Thog and I have been travelling for so long that we can hardly remember what home looks like any more.
First we had to cross the great mountains. There we got caught in a blizzard. It was so cold that I thought we would not survive.

Look after my hens and whatever happens, do not let anyone else steal my old tinder box.

Your friend - Nat the hen keeper

Formal letter

Dear Sir,

I am writing to complain about the items that I bought from your shop last moon-month.

I will be calling at your shop once this adventure is over and expect a refund for these goods.

Yours sincerely,
Nat Treegood

Organisation toolkit for a personal letter

Remember to:

- write **your address** in the **top right** hand part of the page
- write the **date** underneath the address
- start your letter on the **left** hand side of the page. Use an informal greeting (Dear Nat)
- explain why you are writing in the **first sentence**
- set out your letter in **paragraphs**. Start each one on a new line with a **topic sentence**
- **sign off** your letter on a new line
- make your letter **detailed** and **interesting**.

Organisation toolkit for a formal letter

Remember to:

- write **your address** in the **top right** hand part of the page
- write the **date** underneath the address
- write the **address** of the person the letter is for. Write this lower down than the date and on the **left** hand side of the page
- start your letter underneath with a **formal** greeting (Dear Mr Smith; Dear Sir)
- explain **who** you are and **why** you are writing in the **first sentence**
- set out your letter in **paragraphs**. Start each one on a new line with a **topic sentence**
- write about what you want to happen next in your **closing paragraph**
- sign off your letter on a new line (Yours sincerely).

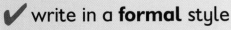

LANGUAGE TOOLKIT

Remember to:

✔ write in a **formal** style
✔ make your letter **clear** and **detailed**.

Writing diaries

Purpose
A diary is for recording events, thoughts and feelings for now and in the future.

Audience
It is usually just for the writer. However, sometimes a diary is read by other people, for example, *Anne Frank's Diary.*

A diary is a **recount**. Remember all the points on the **toolkits** on page 29 and look at the extra toolkits below.

Organisation toolkit
Remember to:
- write the date (and possibly the time) at the start of each entry
- organise your writing into **paragraphs**. These should show the sequence of events and the flow of your thoughts.

LANGUAGE TOOLKIT

Remember to:
- ✔ use the **past tense** to record events and the **present tense** for thoughts and feelings (*I am so excited because ...*)
- ✔ use an **informal style**
- ✔ use **powerful** and **emotive** words and phrases to show your own thoughts and reactions
- ✔ choose words carefully to make **links** between diary entries (*It is five weeks now since ...*).

Biographical writing

Purpose
Autobiographies record the life of the author. **Biographies** record someone else's life.

Audience
Both kinds of writing are for people who are interested in finding out more about the person.

Autobiographies and biographies are examples of **recounts**.

Look at the **toolkits** on page 29 and the extra toolkits lists below.

Organisation toolkit
Remember to:
- write an **introduction** that makes the person sound interesting or unusual
- include family trees, timelines, photographs or pictures with captions
- write a **conclusion** that contains a reflection on the person's life or (if the person is still alive) some hopes or thoughts about the future.

LANGUAGE TOOLKIT

Autobiography
Remember to:
- ✔ write in the **first person**
- ✔ include your **opinions** and **feelings**
- ✔ choose whether to write in a **formal** or **informal** style
- ✔ include **quotes** from people who know you, in direct or reported speech.

Biography
Remember to:
- ✔ write in the **third person**
- ✔ write in a **formal** style
- ✔ include **quotes** from people who knew the person, in direct or reported speech.

Non-fiction

Journalistic writing

The purpose and audience for **journalistic writing** depends upon the kind of article being written and the type of newspaper or magazine it is published in.

Purpose

Newspapers and magazines keep people up to date with news events, provide entertainment and tell people more about subjects that interest them.

+

Audience

Newspapers and magazines usually have a specific **target audience**

Examples of target audiences:

- A local newspaper is for people who live in a certain area.
- A school newspaper is for everyone connected with the school.
- Magazines about different topics,
  e.g. computer games, model-making, music, cooking, gardening) are for people who like these activities.
- Comics are usually for children.

Newspapers and magazines contain:

- news stories
- interviews
- letters
- advertisements
- puzzles
- reports.

Many articles are **mixed text types**.

> **THE DAILY TIMES**
> April 17th 1912
>
> **TITANIC HAS SUNK!**
>
> At 11.40pm on April 14th, the world's largest ocean liner skimmed the side of an iceberg in the Atlantic Ocean. Three hours later she had sunk. Over 1500 people have drowned or been frozen to death in the icy waters.

Organisation toolkit

Remember to:

- include a **masthead** (name of paper), the **date** and a **headline**
- include a **flash** (a one line summary of the contents of the page) (*Over 1500 passangers died when Titanic hit an iceberg*)
- give an **introduction** to sum up the story and interest the reader. This is often in **bold** type
- write in **columns** and use **sub-headings**
- include **pictures** with **captions** and **diagrams**, if relevant
- give a **conclusion** that might include the paper's opinion
- include a **by-line** (the reporter's name).

LANGUAGE TOOLKIT

Remember to:

✔ write in the **third person**
✔ use attention-grabbing language such as powerful **verbs** and **adjectives**, emotive language and short, snappy phrases
✔ use **alliteration**, **rhyme**, **puns** and **word play** in the headlines (*Fall of the Titan*)
✔ include **quotations** from people who saw what happened as **direct** or **indirect speech** (*Eye witnesses report that as the bow section sank, the stern righted itself for a short time*)
✔ use **standard phrases** for anything that is uncertain (*Mr Smith claimed; it is alleged*).
✔ include detail **concisely** ('*People didn't realise what had happened*' said <u>first class passenger</u>, <u>Bridget McDermott, 31</u>).

Informal writing

An **informal style** is rather like conversation. It can be used in:

- diary writing

- letters to friends

- some kinds of persuasive writing such as adverts, fliers and personal opinions

- notes to yourself.

Look at the example from 'Guide to Planet Marco'.

Top of the World

Are you the outdoor type? Do you like to challenge yourself? Get away from the daily routine and travel to one of the most beautiful places in the universe with this tailor-made Mountain Trek on Planet Marco, the red planet.

The spectacular Morstan Mountain Range is one of the great wonders of the universe. The mountains tower more than several miles high but the air is always sweet and breathable. Local guides will lead you through this once-in-a-lifetime journey.

Next >

© Planet Marco Tourist Information   NOTE: SITE STILL UNDER CONSTRUCTION!

LANGUAGE TOOLKIT

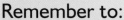

Remember to:

✔ use **colloquial words** and **phrases**

✔ make it sound more like **speech**

✔ make use of **punctuation**, for example, use a dash to show an afterthought or an aside.

Formal writing

A **formal style** is used in many kinds of non-fiction writing, for example:

- explanations
- some non-chronological reports
- some pieces of persuasive writing
- discussions
- business letters.

One of the most important factors in deciding whether to use a formal style is to think about the **task** you are writing and **who** the writing is for. For example, if you are writing to a chairman of a company about a serious complaint, you will need to write formally.

When you write in a formal style, you create a 'distance' between yourself and the reader.

LANGUAGE TOOLKIT

Remember to:

✔ use the **third person**

✔ use the **passive voice** to alter the emphasis in the sentence

✔ choose more **formal connectives** (furthermore, nevertheless, moreover, in addition)

✔ use **formal vocabulary** (enquire/request (ask), respond/response (reply), feature/factor (thing))

✔ write in a way that avoids personal involvement

✔ use **stock phrases** that are 'polite' even though you may be annoyed.

Always think about what you are writing and who is going to read it.

You will often need to decide which features to use in order to write in the correct style for the task.

Editing writing

1. Think about the **writing task**.

   - What sort of writing is it?

   - Who is it for?

   - Have you done what you were asked to do?

   - Will your reader understand it?

2. Look at ways to **improve your sentences**, for example:

   - make words count by changing weak verbs or adjectives

   - make sure that you have a range of sentence types, for example, simple, compound and complex

   - check that you have started sentences in different ways

   - check that you have found different ways of connecting your sentences and ideas

   - edit clumsy sentences, for example, use one word instead of several.

3. Check your **spelling** and **punctuation**. (It is often easier to spot mistakes if you read your work aloud.)